BURNED

BURNED

BURNED

Forwarded by
Dr. Pamela Robinson

Wow! Burned Is A Phenomenal Testimony of Triumph Over Tragedy!...A Powerful Testimony Of A Woman Once Battered, Raped and Abused Emotionally Survive The Unthinkable and Today Is Dedicated to Uplifting and Supporting Men, Women and Children of Abuse, Rape and Domestic Violence transform their lives and change their story from Victim to Victor!

Burned is an unforgettable story that will have you turning page after page and the rioting drama unfolds...So fasten your seat belt, get comfortable as the pages of struggle and a determination to live unfold. into the Great Story of Love and Inner Strength....

Dr. Pamela Robinson

BURNED

BURNED

WARNING

Before you get into the car please put your seat belt on, be aware that the road your about to embark upon is filled with bumpy roads that smooth out as we get closer to Destiny Blvd.

Please leave all judgmental thoughts outside of the car. Don't be afraid to cry, to laugh, to learn, to let go and breathe.

If you need to stop at anytime along the way please feel free and we will do so. It's absolutely ok to have emotions good and bad, but when we come to the end of the road please place it in the garbage bag and throw it away in the garbage can that will be provided for you once you get out.

Now that you have been warned if you need a jacket/scarf/hat/a drink/a box of tissue you can get it now so that we could carry on.

I almost forgot to let you know that if you want to go back and review we can go to the newsroom and search the records at Florida today's news or fox 5, channel 2, channel 13 news.

You will find everything dealing with the molestation as a child, the domestic violence as an adult, my sisters death, and the death of my son. Ok now we can begin...

BURNED

Born into flames and broken pieces.
Abused and misused, by the family she knew and respected along with the outside world.
She never expected to be rejected by some and brutally humiliated by others.

My father wasn't in the pic, maybe because he was a married man and his wife wouldn't be disrespected again with a child from his affairs with his mistress.

She was moved all over and from place to place. She had an array of people to live with an I put emphasis on the different types of personalities she was influenced by. But when she was with her mother it was incredibly deficient.

I had a few good times with my mom, but I felt like an outstanding balance to her that she was trying to pay off.

I never asked to be here, I only wanted to be loved and given affection like anyone else in the world.

BURNED

Dr Jones asked, Are you angry with your mom and the response she gave you growing up?

"Not anymore but I sure used to be, I wanted to rip her to shreds and feed her to the gators. I wanted her to feel the way I did and to hurt and see that I was in critical condition."

It felt like she was so sweet and informational and giving to the world but behind closed doors she was the lock nest monster waiting for an opportunity to write me off, I felt like she was my Joan Crawford.

Her prize possession was stolen from her at the tender age of 5 and destroyed by the one closest to her, that was supposed to love and teach her all the things a father would teach his baby girl since he was now married to her mother and taking on the response ability as her father.

Although she covered it well it was still available to be repeated in her archive of memory. Never could she have imagined this lifestyle that was given to her precious hands and inflicted in her pure heart.
She fought herself daily because she was shoveled the line that," it was her fault" and she better not tell a soul.

"How was it my fault?" she asked in the middle of her story. " I was a baby i never asked him to come in my house and destroy it, so what my skin was flawless and I hadn't been touched by the world of freaks and predictable savage beast like him!"

Burnt from the pain of being entered into time and time again forcefully with no lubrication nor regards of her oppressor and depressor, except for the fact that he had reached his nasty climax. He pulls out of her naked without protection, excited and relived of the stress he encountered from being an adult and dealing with the issues he faced with her mom. The stepfather,"I'm done with you, go back to bed and you better not tell a soul."
Not knowing or even caring he pulls out her voice, life, joy, freedom, power and respect while filling her with fear, doubt, hate, rebellion, low self-esteem, along with the heat of the selfish flames he tortured her with.

A few hours later she hears him and her mom getting into and then boom!
Mommy likes when he does it to her cause she said, "it feels good baby, give me more!" "Both of them must not love me," she cried as she listened to them in the room next to her.

From the age of five to ten she suffered many broken sleeplessness nights filled with negative emotions and suicidal thoughts that brought pure rage to her plate.

She finally got the courage to tell her mom but she didn't believe her. Years later they got a divorce.

Get this he wasn't the only one inflicting pain on me, his brother joined in added his flame to the fire along with another of her mother's flings.

How do you feel about the people that abused you?

"Well honestly, I try not to think about them or what happened. I pray that they asked for forgiveness from God before they died, if they're deceased. "

Dr Jones. Did you forgive them? "Believe it or not I did because it was holding me back. "

Not only was she burnt by her mom's husband and other's.
her mom rejected her and her truth and explained it was some crazy story and that it was all a lie to get attention.

(Dr. Jones) How is your relationship with your mom? "She has her life and I have my own life, I love her to life because carried me for nine months and she didn't have to.

"Wait, did I tell you that mom had been burned also but still lived off of 42nd street and Denial blvd."

Quina and her baby sister play outside like nothing ever happened the night before. Yall come in so you can eat.. Placed on the table on their plates cabbage rice and smothered pork chops...the girls begin to giggle.. What's so funny he asked? We were just laughing at her socks, they don't match. (stepdad) Well hurry up and get done it's almost bath time. Yes Sir.

I want to tell you something Quina her baby sister Tracy whispered.. OK Quina said.

(Stepdad-Roy) Bedtime girls. (the girls yell) Yes sir! The girls get into bed and they say goodnight as he closes the door. Quina goes over to baby's bed as quickly and quietly and asks her what she wanted to tell her.

Baby a 6 year old begin to tell Quina that her dad was trying put his wand in her pocketbook and it was hurting. They both began crying. Shhhhh baby we don't want him to get upset and come in here.

Baby's dad, my stepfather.

My dad said, he would hurt me and you if I told anyone. He told me the same thing.. he's been doing the same thing to me. We have to tell mommy said Quina! No I don't want her to be... her to be what baby? Ok baby.. it will be ok I will find a way to fix it.

As time goes by the brother's of the black tulip begin to take part in Quina when no one is around....

Ok Doc this getting real thick I don't know if I can do this....

What's stopping you Quina? (Dr Jones)

Dude you don't understand, (crying) this hurts... okkkk just let me breathe!!

Ok so this continues I'm not sure at what point we told our mom but it didn't matter cause the saga continued until baby was around 6 and then the garbage hit the fan! Excuse my language doc.... so as it would happen that the black tulip struck again but this was the night our lives changed, after bath time my sister ran to mom and she was bleeding from her pocketbook.

All I can remember is yelling and screaming and mommy running down the hall with the knife next stop was emergency room and then me and baby going to this old lady house..

Miss Moss was our new mommy for the time we with her. The lady (Bonita Codswell) that took us to her house said, girls we need you to stay here until we find out what happened to you both and get mom some help. She told me and baby we were going to be safe here and nobody was gonna hurt us again.

Just imagine the pain of being a little child as a grown man inserts his power into her small voice box... it's like having Goliath stand over you abusing his authority and injecting you with his power drill. The sad part is he doesn't care about your tears he just wants to reach his peak.

Miss Moss had a beautiful house and plenty of food. Miss Moss said that she would take great care of until our mommy can get us. That night baby wet the bed cause she was scared. Miss Moss didn't like that but baby couldn't help it she was scared. I don't think the old lady understood it cause she seemed so angry. Baby wet the bed every day. I told baby everything was going to be fine and we could go home as soon as they get her help..
The system burned us because we spent Christmas at the department of children and family services office...

They told us that we couldn't go home until our mommy left Roy... well we stayed there for a year. Burned again....

We meet so many nice people and we went to a good school... On weekends we went different places and we went to her other daughters house. Omg she was a teacher and me and baby thought they were rich because all of the beautiful things that she had. Her house was filled with so many beautiful items and she had so many clothes and shoes for us to play dress up. She was really nice to us.

We always had great food and fun. The carrot salad was best..oh yeah the chocolate cake and greens and macaroni and cheese were so delicious! This is were I learned how to cook macaroni and cheese. We had bikes baby dolls and everything we ever dreamed about.

They had a church we went to, we had sleep overs and coloring books, crayons books and everything a little girl could want, we baked cookies, cake, we learned to cook different things, it was just amazing but we were still burned.

After a while baby didn't wet in the bed every night.. Miss Moss had a huge backyard and front yard that we played in all the time. She lived on the corner. We made friends with the neighbors, I was scared because I knew that one day I would leave them too. Oh I almost forgot, some of the people I went to church with lived across the street from miss Moss and I would get to see them and play with them.

BURNED

As time goes on we finally got to go back to our mom...When we went back we had to go to counseling and talk about what happened again and again... it was so much happening in our lives that some things were hard to understand as children.

However as a child I do remember going from place to place and staying with my aunties and uncles and grandparents.
Now that burned me cause as soon as I got settled we moved again.

I did spend some time with my grandparents in SC.. It was always great at my grandparents. They were great cooks and examples of love, peace and joy. I remember when they took us to king's dominion theme park in Virginia, and when we went to Chimney Rock Mountain in Asheville N.C.
We did so many cool things, for example going for Sunday drives, having ice cream after church, looking at Christmas lights, skating on Monday nights watching wrestling on Saturday morning's. Going to the radio station that he owned. I mean it was absolutely incredible.

I remember my grandmother was my teacher in preschool or kindergarten. I remember her letting me GE chocolate milk for lunch. I think it was preschool because we went to the basement of the church where we were taught our ABC'S and things. I used to think my grandmother was white because her skin collection is so bright and beautiful.

My grandparents loved each other so much. Looking back they were the first example of a relationship. I never ever heard them yelling or screaming at each other. I never saw tension between them or anything negative.. Burned every time I left them....

(Dr. Jones) So how'd that make you feel?

(Quina) Great because I wanted to be like them a feel what they felt.
(Dr. Jones) So you were around 11 or 12 right Quina? Yes...

(Dr. Jones) So even at such a young age you understood that what they had you wanted. (Quina)absolutely Doc!

As time goes by other people engaged in you right Quina asked, Dr. Jones?

BURNED

Ok Dr. I'll be back tomorrow! Quina grabs her purse and walks hastily out the door and slammed it!
Dr Jones calls out to Quina to no avail....

Dr. Jones sits back in his chair and says (my God let your healing process begin...) he finishes his paper work up and puts his Grey trench coat along with his Grey brim and scarf and goes outside and gets into his back Lincoln navigator and goes home.

After her session with Dr. Jones Quina went to Red lobster and ate a basket of biscuits, steak along with some shrimp pasta with some freshly steamed broccoli on the side and some sweet tea. When she was finished she left her $5 tip on the table and left.

The Dr walks into his office around 8am dressed in navy blue pin striped pants with a sky blue dress shirt on, tireless with a navy trench and brim... he smelled like Georgo Armani he goes to the front desk and asks the secretary for his mail and notes.

Good morning Dr Jones, give me one second as she prepares his request. As the Dr walks away he says,"thanks Miss Ann."

Quina walks into the office at 10am signs in. Miss Ann said, "the Dr will be with you in a minute." Meanwhile Quina sits down and Dr. Matthew walks in and asks Miss Ann if she could call and see if the local garden center had any fresh lilies.

Quina you can come in now said Dr. Jones. Quina gets up with her navy blue orange bottom shoes black pencil skirt along with her navy blue shirt and navy blue pinstripe scarf and navy blue petticoat, with a navy handbag.

Quinn sits down on the chase as she greats Dr. Jones. Morning Dr. J. I want to apologize for the way I walked out yesterday it was just way to much to process. Say Doc did you know that I could prove my story? What do you mean Quina? Well it just happened to be in the newspapers and on TV in Florida... I mean I believed you anyway but it does bring some validity to your story.

Dr. Jones replies, it's ok Quina I understand. So let's get back to where we left off.

BURNED

Yes Dr. Jones Besides my stepfather and his brother's along with another an officer who used to work for the police department in Cocoa. He and mamma were well I can't really explain they relationship but he also took part in destroying my self esteem... thanks for lying to my mom and destroying the little relationship with her we did have..

Man CJ, I thought you loved us.. You really messed me up. You just used us, how could you not tell the truth? Now by this time I learned that no matter what I want, I had no choice but to do as I was told because no one would ever believe me. I don't know what the men were seeing in me but I hate that they took so much from me...

Oh yeah they're was one girl that took a part in my life when I was about 4 or 5 years old. No one ever knew about that. Her name was
Tonya...
I was down the street at my aunt O house with my cousins at the time, spending time with them when she took a slice of my pie....

Unfortunately there are two main characters in my life that I for some strange reason I look up too took part in the drainage of my soul... If I tell you who it would destroy a lot of innocent people that I definitely don't want to expose....

(Quina) Dr. Jones it's so darn sad that I learned to lie and cover hurt at the early stages of my life, but I understand that it's a process that we all have to deal with something in one form or another...

"Dr. Jones", I completely understand. It's clearly the responsibility of the adults to make sure that the children are well taken care of to the best of their ability. In most cases it's a pattern because the parents more than likely have dealt with the same issue's. They know your telling the absolute truth because they know the signs and symptoms and are afraid to speak up or out.

Ok my dear would you like to take a quick break and get some fresh air? Once you get back we will have 30 more minutes and we'll call it quits for the day.
Ok Dr Jones as she picks up her belongings and walks out the door.

BURNED

She goes across the street to Dairy Queen and purchases a banana split with all chocolate ice cream along with pineapple slices strawberries and nuts with chocolate syrup drizzled over the entire Sunday....I forgot the bananas... omg Quina said, " this was incredible! This has to be heaven".... just incase you didn't know Quina loved herself some ice cream and ice...

The Dr asks his secretary Mrs.. Anne for a cup of coffee. As she prepares his coffee he goes back in his office and reflects on what the day has been like after he reads his notes.

Dr Matthew knocked on Dr Jones's door and asked him, hey doc have you heard about the book Love Device's? He replied, oh yes doc I gotta copy waiting on me at home. I plan on reading it this weekend. I already told my wife that I was going to spend some time reading it this weekend while she was out. I have been looking at the reviews and since the guys a new author I'd give him a try. Plus he had me at Love Device's.

Dr. Matthew replied I just ordered mine 3 days ago and I'm excited about reading it. You know I met the guy that wrote it last week. He briefly explained it to me and some other people because he was doing a book signing at Walmart on Lawrenceville highway...

He was a very passionate young man and he was super excited about his material....

As the office door opens the chimes go off. Ok doc time for my next client as Dr. Matthew walks towards the door. I catch up with you later.

Ok, please send Quina in for me. No problem.

Miss Quina Dr. Jones is ready for you now. Thanks she said as she passes him.

Ok Quina are you ready to finish up for weekend, said Dr. Jones?

Sure Doc let's move on....
Hey doc did I ever tell you that when I was around four that I loved to hula hoop? Dr. Jones - no you didn't.

BURNED

Well when I was younger my mom would tell everyone that her baby could hula hoop like no one's business. I was so good at it and everyone wanted me to do it all the time. I remember at my 4th birthday party having a hula hoop party and everyone watching me.

My mom had the biggest brightness smile on her face with that ponytail and scarf wrapped around the ponytail. She had some big fancy shades on because we were outside and it was the greatest party ever.. and I had so much fun. I had a lot of gifts. Now listen I don't want you to misjudge my mother because she's had a lot of things happen in her life. I don't blame her because I know she did her best...

(Dr. Jones) It's ok Quina, I'm 'm not hear to judge your mom I'm hear to help you.
I think it's a good time to end for the week.
We can start fresh next week.

Ok sounds like a great idea. I'll see you on Tuesday next week at 3pm Dr. J. Ok have a great weekend.... Will do and you do the same as she walks out the door...

Quina walks out the office to her car and turns on her radio on to her favorite song.. life is a highway and I'm going to ride it all night long! She gets on Broadway and stays on it till she gets home.

To those that have been where I was and to those dealing with this situation. Your life is not over. You can become whole again. It's many ways for you to deal with the pain of the empty needle going into your heart killing you instantaneous.

BURNED

Whatever you do it's very important for you to get and find your healing and own it because you deserve it and it belongs to you. Once you get your healing never allow anyone to take it from you again. People will try everything and anything to get you off balance but you have to hold on no matter what life brings to you or your doorsteps.

The most important thing for you to do is seek help from your physician, then get into therapy with a real therapist not your local church counselor. A lot of people will go to the church because they feel a sense of comfort but it doesn't always work like that most of the time they are the ones that will use what you say against you and try to get you to do sex acts for them. Now listen I'm not saying all counselors are the same
You just have to decide what is right for you.

And to all my ladies that have children please be aware of the fact that you could be sleeping with the enemy. Especially when they seem more interested in your child than you. One major thing I learned as a child is to never allow a man to beat your child with no lubrication. What I mean is never allow them to be spanked, beaten butt naked.
I remember being beaten butt naked after I got out of the bathtub. I would get tied to the bed and then my mom would stuff a rag in my mouth. Now being 5,6,7 I can't fathom what a child could do to be treated like an animal? But life goes on and we must be aware of everything we do, say and what we allow to go on and through in your life.

BURNED

Part 2

As she approaches her home she slows down to turn in the drive and parks the car. She gets out and goes inside through the family room. She calls out bae, I'm home... he greets her with a kiss as she approaches the living room.
How was your day he inquires as they sit down. It was good and yours? Same here. So how did it go with Dr. Jones this time? She lays her head on his lap and he runs his fingers through her head as she explains that it all went well and it was a great idea to go back and see him again.

I'm so happy that you placed your fears on the table and went in. You know the whole world could benefit from counseling. I just want you to get better and to understand what makes you tick as a individual. He kisses her forehead gently as she responds thanks ba.

I have one more week then I'll be done with the counseling sessions... Congratulations ba I'm extremely happy for you. You know ba I have been through so much in my life at times it's hard for me to express myself. I certainly don't understand how you deal with all my baggage. The crazy part of all this it's all been televised and in the news papers, well the major ones was recorded.

Now listen we all have past and I can't judge you because I was sent to love you past your pain and into your future.

So what is for dinner tonight bae Since it's the weekend and we both have had a long week, I ordered red lobster for us. Quina squeezed him and said you always know what I want.

He said, I should know everything about you... girl you know your my best friend...

BURNED

Ok.... I have a confession.... as Quina gets up off his lap she said well baeI kinda cheated on you today and he said okay Quina what did you do this time? Well I, I, I had desert already, I went to Dairy Queen and I had a good old fashioned banana split!

You dirty little scoundrel you... Girl you are so cute! I knew it... I saw you when I passed by on my way downtown..
Now you get up and let me run your shower 0ur food should be here by the time you finish. Ok (Quina)

They get up he grabs her belongings and they go to the room she begins to get undressed as he runs her shower... she said thanks Sugarbear, as he walked out the room the door bell rings he yells out just a minute please....

He gets to the door and opens it. The delivery guy says good evening Sir nice to see you again. He replied good to see you again how are things going? Good sir, enjoy your meal. T hank's.

He closes the door and begins to set up the dinner on the coffee table. He puts on old school music... Quina calls out to him ba is that old school? You know it he responds. I'm on my way hold it down for me big guy! I got you covered beautiful!

As Quina enters the room filled with flowers she says no way you got me this time!

Sugarbear were are you? As she scanned the room she sees him behind the roses. He walks up to her hand her the flowers and kisses her forehead and says come on and let's eat and watch this movie beautiful. But how did you do all this so fast? It wasn't fast it took about 20 minutes.... now come on our lobster is waiting on us... as he turns the music off and turns the movie on..

BURNED

So Quina sits down as he begins to serve her and says awwww I love you so much Sugarbear!

Ba this is great! He replied one day I'll take you to Maine for some real lobster right out the water.... that sounds like fun, I'm down for that!

He gets up and turns the TV off, Quina runs to the room and says, " the last one is a rotten egg "..he follows , no way he dives into the bed...not fair Quina crys, "you always get me." Sugarbear reaches over and says, " awwww my sweetheart it's ok... kisses her forehead and says good night big water head.." and lays down.

Saturday morning before Quina gets up Tony gets up and makes breakfast for her and he calls out to her and says, "wake-up sleeping beauty.." Quina slowly rolls over and looks at the clock and says are you serious its 11 am. She said, "what did you cook good looking?" He replied, "breakfast silly."

Ok let me wash my face and brush my teeth. She returns to bacon eggs and toast with some orange juice.

Tony asked her what she wanted to do today and she replied, "I just want to chill and begin to work on my book."
Sounds like a plan beautiful. He began to tell her about his book signing and how it went and how thankful he was that he had the opportunity to do it..

Meanwhile on the other side of town. Dr Jones sat down to start reading Love Device's. He took plenty of notes even though the book wasn't very long., he took about 2 hours with it.

BURNED

Wow this was great! Then his wife enters his study and asks how was he as they walked towards each other to embrace. He responds oh babe I'm fine. I just got done reading this incredible short book. She asked if she could see it he said sure as he picked the book she said oh wow I have been hearing so much about this young man and his wife ,both of them have incredible books out. At that moment the door bell rung she said it's my sister I'll be back, she went and answered the door and they began to laugh and giggle they passed the study on the way to the den and the sister Liz yelled out hey big brother...
He replied heyyyyy!

He went over and turned on his radio on to his jazz station and danced his way to his lounge chair and sat down and fell fast asleep....
He was awoken with the sweet smells coming from the kitchen around 6pm.
Hey Hun you hungry?

Yessssss, it smells great what are you cooking up he asked?
Some asparagus with located baked potatoes and steak, give me a minute and I'll be back!

Back at Quina and Tony's they are enjoying some BBQ chicken and Spanish rice. They are making plans for the next phase of their life as they enjoy their dinner.

Early Sunday morning Quina and Tony get ready for Church... and Quina asked Sugarbear what he wanted for dinner? he replied how about some spaghetti and sweet tea? Quina said sure as long as you fix it the way you did the first time you did for me lol... you know how much I love your spaghetti.

BURNED

Alright, you got it.... I'll get the meat out the deep freezer. On the way going to church Quina said, " I can't wait for you to cook dinner Ba"...

He responds by saying it will be even better than before.... and smiles...

After church they stopped at Walmart and aldi's to get the rest of the ingredients for dinner and off to Spaghetti wasted...

On the way home Tony said Momma preached today. Quina replied with Apostle Pamela Ogguin taught today baby! She wasn't playing no games! The spell breaker was a delicious word! When I say this woman walked through fire and rain, she tore down the streets of strongholds, and went on the mountain tops to break the chains of bondage! You can tell the she is truly anointed by God and you can feel the drips of oil pour out of her skin it's amazing! She has a beautiful spirit and a beautiful heart, said Tony. Quina replied with, I had her first and I'm not going to let you take her. Lol, she's my Momma too! "Sorry", said Quina, but like I said, she belongs to me! They both began to laugh and say well I guess we can share...

BURNED

Quina and Sugarbear returned home and both changed clothes and got comfortable. Ok ba I'm going to fix supper do you need anything?
No thanks I'm going to get back to my book until dinner is ready...

Dinner took about 45 minutes for him to prepare for us y'all and when I tell you dinner was everything and some..This man is so freaking incredible and I wouldn't give him up for anything in this world! He puts his everything in everything he does for me. He has to have a heart of pure and unselfish love and devotion for me. I never knew that I could receive love like this... Yall this man is unlike any other man I've ever known.

Hes everything I prayed for, he's a gentle giant, very respectful, understanding, affectionate, passionate, humble, outgoing, intelligent, inspiring, dedicated, determined, detailed, strong, confident, courageous, giving, I could go on and on but I'll just stop here. Oh yeah not to mention that this man can cook his socks off... His food took to my stomach and wouldn't let me go.

BURNED

I just have to tell y'all that you have to be patient when it comes to relationships. Yessssss, I said it... sometimes you have go through to find that out.. Listen take my advice about relationships so you don't make the same mistakes I did..

The first thing you have to do is pray about it and ask for directions.... never get married because you get pregnant, never let someone force you into it, never get married at a young age, please make sure that it's what both of you want......never do it on a whim, make sure you both legitimately love each other and it's no puppy love... make sure you have given it plenty of thought and time...

Please don't do it because you're missing out on your father's love.....

Now listen my first marriage was hell on a ledge waiting for the cookies to crumble and cookie monster to come and get the crumbs. Six of the most beautiful children came from this unequally yoked desert storm...

BURNED

Now let me just sit this here before we get into the next phase of misery loves misery with chocolate ice cream and chopped pineapples, strawberries, strawberry syrup and chocolate syrup with the cherry on top. As the world turns and the burrito gets burned.

Father missing in action hiding in his flakey crust that he made himself in a drunken struggle with super dark shades on. I seriously thought he wasn't around because I wasn't good enough, pretty enough, smart enough or I had done something tremendously wrong.

I came to the conclusion that it had nothing do with me, as I got older I realized that he had a different family on the other side of the stormy rain clouds.

Yes other children were involved. I'm not totally sure but I think it's 6 others... I have a good relationship with one of my brothers and one of my sisters, I could be better but..

I really need to be honest about the situation, I'm just not a really good communicator and haven't completely communicated with everyone like I should but I feel like if they wanted to be a part of my life they would open the front door and asked me if I would like a seat and a cold coke with a plate of fresh fried chicken wings and or chicken legs with collard greens and neck bones, white rice, corn bread and cabbage. And to top it off a slice of sweet potato pie.

Now as I understand him and my siblings had great working relationships...they knew each other well and they lived in the same area. I was just an outsider that got none of his dang time, affection, support or even love... this was complete nonsense to me....

BURNED

How dare this man, a deacon in the church... This man really messed up a part of my life. I just wanted to be loved, nurtured, supported and respected but I didn't get it.... I just wanted to belong somewhere, to fit in like other people I saw. I just wanted love in the purest form.

Thank God for my Granddaddy. He showered me with all the things I was missing from my biological donor.

Burned again cause it was a temporary fix... My grandfather passed when I was in my early 20's... What in the world?

I really feel like if I had a father's love, support and correction I wouldn't have served 20 years of my life in San Quentin...

Just kill yourself, why don't you?

Burned but officially not our fault but back to the house of the unknown man who completely abandoned me without a cause, just the mental disorder I was left with....

Now I remember seeing him once as a teenager and he came through the desert to see me get married the first time and that was it. Never any consistency in my life just a lot of old sob stories and lies. Even as I grew older he never tried to communicate with me. He still hasn't tried to repair the bridge that stopped him from being my father. He hasn't even apologized for leaving me and my mom dangling off the bridge. I feel like he committed selfish acts and just didn't give a dang as to how we would eat or live or the sacrifice my mom had to make to take care of me whether it was buying shoes clothes or food for me and her. Or how she was going to educate me and how she would make sure I was in extra cariclal activities. Just by the grace of God I had aunts and uncles who helped along the way even my grandparents to provide me with love unconditionally.

BURNED

even know what married life entailed...
I actually thought it was a relationship with love, holding hands, affection, romance, paying bills, going on trips with the family, enjoying great fooI do remember asking what happened between him and my Joan Crawford, his response was, that's non of your business. I knew what my mom said about him, I just wanted to know why he didn't sick around for me.

I felt like I had a right to know why this poor excuse of a man left us without any type of financial support or physical or emotional support.

Alright here we go... my time in prison...

At times day was night and night was day. Now don't get me wrong it was good and bad days but the bad outweighed the good days..

We were completely opposite, we really didn't know what we wanted, ok let me just speak for myself. We got married when I was 17....

I didn't know what I really wanted in life or from life. I didn't really and conversation being involved in the local church and community.. like my grandparents did.....

Instead I found myself in lock down... playing cards with the warden.

In the beginning I thought he was my savior. I thought he would provide protection from all the people who had ever hurt and potentially hurt me physically and emotionally.

However I was wrong..
in fact I participated in my life of INSTABILITY, including insanity, self deprivation and low self esteem. I had no control of Quina. Now just because he was older I gave him control and followed his direction and gave him the desires of his black heart occasionally.

BURNED

He took creative control over everything that I said and did.

I told you to kill yourself so you wouldn't have to deal with this crazy storm or man...

Hold on, I have to recover from this dang glass drinking cup he threw at the center of my back... This hurts so bad, no I'm not bleeding this time..... just burned...

Now this was my fault because I wasn't listening to his BS. So he said. Every time some adverse consequences happened it was because I wasn't listening or following his direction.

The main thing is that you are taught as a child is to love, honor and obey your husband.. but what happens when they don't respect you or love you like Christ love the church? All hell breaks out and you loose all respect and it causes you to become bitter and you eventually lose every once of love and respect for them.

I went through a a lot within this salvageable relationship. And it was a train wreck waiting to happen. I think he felt like he had total control because he was older and I gave away my power for protection. Not a great exchange.

I quickly learned that it wasn't worth saving because you can't teach an old do new tricks. He was set in his way and nothing you'd say to him would make a difference. He was a know it all type of person and one that didn't really respect women or how they felt it was more of do what I say mentally because I know more than you. He would change momentarily but right back to the stern drill Sargent.

BURNED

Non affectionate, hated hugs, holding hands.... I had to tell him say your hair looks good to the girls or your dress is pretty or you look nice today or your suit looks good son to the boys. I remember me and the boys hiding in the laundry room or bathroom so I could give them a haircut. I admit when I ask you to do something more than twice and I have the ability to do it and you don't I'll go ahead and do it myself. So I started cutting the boy's hair. He hated to admit it but the more I cut the better I got. I really enjoyed it anyway. I absolutely hate when someone tells me I can't do something because it makes me want to go harder and go all the way in.

How do you think I felt as a grown woman asking for permission to go to different places.. I had to ask if I could take my kids to the park, or other places. No matter where I went he would call to see if I was were I said I was going or he'd come to the location and see what I was doing.

Heaven forbid if I didn't do what I said I was going to do.
He didn't want me to spend no time with his mother, siblings, shoot for that matter anyone he wasn't cool with. His own pastor or wife wasn't able to come over when he wasn't around. He didn't even want me around my own family.
He said he had to hear our conversations to make sure nothing was said out of the way.
burned...

I mean I gave this dude so much control and so much of my life it was Banana's! He was a very controlling and selfish person....

I remember having to sit in the car at the Econo Lodge while he was working and we also sat at Burger King on Merritt Island. Trust me it wasn't easy especially since I had small children.

BURNED

There were times when I would rebel and I'd leave only to let him back in cause I felt sorry for his sorry butt, he would get up in front of the church and told everyone how badly he felt and how much he missed his family and wanted to be with them, dude had no shame or respect for the house of God. This was the only way people would know that I left him... burned because everyone knew my business...

I remember after the twins he took me by my ponytail and drug me across the floor because I didn't give him the answer he wanted and it left a scar in the middle of my head... That's when I started cutting it...
If I didn't have any hair to pull it was great for me....

The only people that knew about the scar was the my hair stylist.... this is why I would always have a short or low cut.

BURNED

Even the time he raped me in the apartment we lived in that his cousin gave us. I don't remember the name of the apartment but it was in Florida and on the second floor.

Yessssss I said rape.... its rape when you say no and the other person still proceeds. Check the law for yourself! We tore that room up fighting cause I didn't want to have sex with him at that point in time... burned again...

He won that night and I became pregnant with baby 5. I faced so much pain and emotional loss in this place.

I thought he really loved me but he didn't show me love... he never wanted to hold hands hug or show me any affection. He just wanted complete control and for me to be a robot that followed his every command when he said.

Now for those that didn't know what was happening behind closed doors I'm glad cause I didn't want you to know what was going on and it wasn't any of your business anyway. The dark blue eye shadow should have told you everything..

I remember the time he bit me in the face... I stayed in the house for at least a week until it healed. I was like in a battle with a wilder beast... This really blew my mind and punched my selfestem right in the stomach.

Then there were the times when he'd choked me until I passed out... I'm so glad God didn't allow me to die in the midst of all this foolishness.....

No one that I could ever remember sat me down and explained what a true relationship was about, what to expect from your partner, nor the art of compromise or that you must have strong communication along with love and respect for each other and individually. It should always be a team effort and not one controlling the other. Marriage is a relationship not war!

BURNED

Let me address the non believers and the ones that would say I can't believe it....

First of all everyone has multiple faces that they put on just like a wolf in sheep's clothing.

No one will ever show everything and every side of themselves... I learned this the hard way.... then there was the time we were visiting his oldest sister and my shirt button came open and I didn't realize it and he started taking trash... I remember the hotel key in the laundry and the red lace panties in the bed....

Now this isn't about me bashing anyone but it's me letting go and dealing with every issue in my life so that I could move forward in my life. Now if you're offended or a non believer then....it is what it is but this is my story and my truth.... I spent over 20 years in prison you didn't....

One of His older sisters would sneak over when he wasn't home and helped me take care of the children. Well for that matter just about everyone that wasn't aloud at the house or I wasn't aloud to be around came and helped me out and I'm truly grateful.... that meant that he thought he had full control but he apparently didn't. God knew I needed help especially after my c-section.

I had so many complications with my pregnancies I had to have help, he wasn't unless I had to keep being a pest..

BURNED

Since I was driving all the time I would cut cost to get my hair and nails done... I would save money up like nothing. I'd have people come over to get their hair done while he was at work and the kids knew what I was doing but no one ever said a word cause I'd always get them something and I'd always make sure they were occupied. Sometimes they would watch me work and even got me things I needed things like water or whatever. I played the game to survive...

All I knew was the church and serving God along with the people. That's what I learned from my grandparents and my mom when she really decided to dedicate her life totally to the Ministry.

I remember her going overseas, taking food and clothing to help others. Now as a preteen I really didn't understand why she did it but later I did.

My life gradually became one of a helping hand.

No matter what I did in my own local church, his comments were you just have to be the center of attention.

I partcipated in everything I could in the church just to get a breather from his selfishness. I participated in the dance Ministry, drama Ministry and helped with Sunday school, even the food, toys for tots, parade and wherever I was needed. Everyone could vouch for the fact that me and my kids were always in church. Even his family that he didn't socialize with on a regular basis...

I remember cutting tires, pouring bleach on his clothes when I got fed up, but I wasn't fed up enough to take my kids and walk away from him because he always told me that no man wanted a woman with a house full of children and no one would ever love me the way he loved me. He would often say that I couldn't survive without him..... wrong answer!

BURNED

Please don't do what I did because in the end karma will have full control. You can never do wrong and get away with it. You will eventually have to pay the consequences for your actions. When you really think about it it's not worth wasting your time or your energy, just walk away.

He knew my life story but he apparently didn't care cause he countuied to add to the ruffled pages of my history...

I finally realized after taking self inventory that it he couldn't give me what I wanted and needed. What I really needed and wanted was my father's love and support but he couldn't give it to me or anyone else cause like me he was burned at some point in his life and he didn't know how to share with anyone else. I mean how could he possibly love me if he didn't love himself.
Think about if really loved himself he would have really loved me like I was him.

Can you believe that I fell for them lame movie lines? Unfortunately I did until I found out who I was and I could do and be anything I wanted to.

I asked God for strength to get out of death valley and he provided me with a way of escape, opened doors I couldn't for myself, created available spaces for me and my children. It didn't happen overnight but it did!

I realized my first husband had to have been burned at some point in his life as well and he never spoke about it with anyone but that didn't give him the right or a reason to burn me....

Life is what you make it you don't have to repeat others mistakes or inflict your garbage bag on someone else.

BURNED

How can you say you loved someone but you speak negativity about them to others and when they move on with they're life you try and ruin their new relationship with negative words accusations and tear them down. To me that means you didn't have no love for them. Why would you be so impulsive and try to destroy their character? I get it hurt people hurt people. Remember it takes two to tango. Don't be so quick to burn your bridges you never know if you will need that person you spit on. Beyond that you have to take responsibility for your actions and leave the other person in hands of God.

I've been burned so many times in my life and never wanted to see others go through what I went through. A lot of times I hid my pain from the world and beyond. Being burned time after time you learn to deal with it internally and keep pushing.

I mean God gave me a complete overhaul... my confidence came back, I learned my worth and what I wanted out of life... I have my two big sister's, to thank for that... Von and Janet. They pushed me beyond my limits and didn't give up on me... they showed me how to be strong and how to function by myself and how to love me and how to treat myself with or without a man. The let me know that I matter and I was worth being loved.
They helped build my esteem back up and taught me how to use my voice and not to be a pushover. I received excellent cooking tips and at times I would get pissed of and be like I know what I'm doing and who are the they to tell me what to do.. listen I really did need the advice. I just thought I was grown and I would figure it out on my own. I'm so grateful that they took the time to pour into me so much wisdom and knowledge. I'm extremely grateful for these two chicks.
I could go on and on with the lessons but I'll stop right here...

The church had a huge impact on my life as well... I had some great leaders in the ministry during that time..

BURNED

God had promised me a good relationship and I wasn't about to go down without his promise. God has been so good to me Quina, he has kept me from killing myself on so many occasions, he stopped me from killing him , he never allowed me to get involved with drugs, prostitution, other women, he kept me from aids and so much more.

My story could have ended in prison on death row for killing this dude, the psychiatric hospital for numerous reasons but God!

He kept his promise to me and in my early 30's blessed me with the most amazing man this side of heaven!

BURNED

I mean we went through to get to each other but it was truly worth it.

I had dreams ambitions, goals, desires, I didn't want to be mediocre and in the first relationship I felt cramped in a box full of Kleenex. I knew that in my heart I was bigger than the box I was locked in trying to get out.. but listen you both have to be on the same page and working together. You can't let anyone block your light or turn your life off. Sometimes you just gotta shine by yourself....

Now a lot of things that happens to us because we're asleep at the wheel and we give total control to the passenger or the crossing guard. Sometimes we just absolutely have no choice or control of our lives, we depend on others to control our stopping and starting.

BURNED

BURNED

Part 3

I lost some keynote speakers on my journey to find myself. As I came out of the garbage bag filled with negativity that the world around me filled over my head made me come to tears and terms with who I am, am not, it seriously separated me from who I was going to be and becoming the woman without the mask on...

Murder was the case I was faced with...
My sister closed her eyes and left me behind to deal with her painful departure, it was unbelievable and unbearable.... for so long I kept asking why her? How dare this clown tell me to get over it, yes he had the nerve to tell me to stop crying so much and get it together.... he never once held me and said we will get through this together....

This was my blood, my baby sister.. we went through the gates of hell and back once it broke and burned us!
Some people have no respect or don't even know love or how to love. I completely ignored his stupidity and continued to lay her to rest.. I mean dang as if her being murdered by the people she thought were her friends wasn't enough here he comes with his insensitivity....

Now you can kill yourself and no one will ever miss you! Your kids would be better off without you! I know you want to be with your sister, I can help you if you leave the key under the doormat...

She was the most loving, kindhearted person I had ever grown to love beyond anything. Her smile lit my world and pushed me to break the chains and stand up for myself... She made me identify with my identity....she believed in my worth and my strength.

BURNED

We shared so much of life and our goals and dreams. She was always getting me dressed for my success, she walked on water just like Peter.....

She wanted me to be great, from the purchase of a handbag at Penney to the purchase of a notebook, ok sis you got this, you can do it! The days I wanted to give up she said, get up and go get it...

The killer laughed in our faces in August 2006....

BURNED

BURNED

And then along the way sweet aunt met cancer and faught it with the courage of David. Although Goliath thought he won when they met he was sadly mistaken because she knew how to pray her way through and around the walls of Jericho!

From day one until she closed her beautiful chocolate eyes our love for each other grew stronger and stronger... She believed in me and every time we would talk she had a scripture for every hurdle I crossed and would cross.

Q you can do all things through Christ Jesus that gives you strength. Q be still and know he is God... Q greatness is your portion!
Q you will make it you weren't born to fail..

Q you were chosen by God for greatness... no matter the situation or how I felt she would always give me affirmation. She would always call me Q instead of Quina.

Oh how I miss you my sweet aunt/ mom/ best friend/sister/girlfriend

BURNED

At times she would feed me chocolate cake and ice cream other times it would be rice eggs and bologna... she also had a mean pan of BBQ chicken and pigs foot..

She would often say you can have whatever your heart desires,   just say what you want and it's yours!

We could talk about absolutely everything and anything because it was a judgment free zone. She never judged me and taught me not to be judgmental and give everyone a chance until you saw them changing masks on you... And then I got a very disturbing call,
Quina she's gone.

No, no, no! You know how much she loves you and how special you are to her... but why? She was tired and she wanted peace and rest.

"It's ok Quina," Sugarbear said. "I'm here for you and I'm not going anywhere."

So once you come along I loose my comfort and my strength? Just the opposite because she is still alive and well in your heart. She just waited until I was by your side to comfort and care for you.. She was finally at peace because we have each other.

She wanted to make sure you were free and fine before she left here.. But it still hurts so freaking bad, listen I got you! I'm so glad you're here Sugarbear...

Now I know that I'm all over the place but just sit back and ride with me till the end...

BURNED

Even before the first failed relationship I would pray and ask God to deliver me and to allow me a second chance at a real relationship. I had it all figured out in myself what I wanted and needed.

I wanted a strong man with traits of my grandfather and my Bishop. Now Bishop was like a father to me. I could rely on him and have conversations like a father would with his daughter. Hold up burned again because he didn't belong to me...

I know it sounds crazy but fasten your seat belts.

I wanted a man that wouldn't put his hands on me to hurt me physically but in a most respectful way. A man that would hold my hands and my heart in high regards. A man that would take my hands and pray for and with me no matter the time day or night or even 3 or 4 am.

I wanted a man that would worship with me and not play with God!
I wanted a man that wouldn't be ashamed to hold me in public or just sitting at home watching TV. I wanted a man that wouldn't let me go pass the border built around the waterfront. I wanted a man that would be our strength in the wilderness and the darkest cliffs. I needed and wanted a man that knew when I needed to rest and who could take care of me in sickness and health just as I would be for him.

I wanted a man that could cook for me and my children, a man that would be my equal. One who was responsible and reliable and well respected every where he went. One that was very inspiring and intelligent and creative.
One that would love me past my pain and imperfections, one who was respectful. One that had girls for me to love on and do there hair and makeup and play dress up with. Simply because that's what I have always loved to do with my girls. I honestly wanted to have more children with someone I loved and appreciated and admired, and they felt the same way about me.... One that would love my children like his own.

BURNED

One that would take us in and change our world, one who would speak life over us all, one who would pray until he reached heaven and one who would minister the word like he lost his mind. A man that would and could seek the face of God without shame or fear... a man that could here from God and fared God.

A great all around great human being that I could support and submit to. I did ask for a 6ft man that I could look up to and one that would hold me, squeeze me and love me like I never felt before. And the cherry on top was that he had to have a smell that was unforgettable and I would know him by his aroma...

Now it took some time for us to meet up but it was well worth it when we did, i was in my early 30's when meet. I couldn't believe it, he was everything I wanted and needed in my life..

For the most part everyone was extremely excited for me when he came into my heart after my triple bypass surgery.

He helped with the healing process and began the building process!... He gave me his heart and soul mind and body along with everything he owned. Married March 24th, 2012..

Now as we travel through the desert and rain forests we have shared highs and lows with the people in the garden trying to transform us into the people they wanted us to become.

We meet on stage and we were completely challenged with the belief of others. So many loved our stage presence and others said we had to choose the stage or Ministry...

BURNED

Of course we choose the Ministry over the stage but the stage is were our hearts and passions lay. By choosing the Ministry it felt like a part of our love had been taken away from us, well me. No both of us.

All the players that have been along the road with thought I had lost my mind... Now the whole time I was in World of faith I was able to use all of my gifts dance, acting, speaking, poetry it was never a choice between the gifts. I was taught that your gifts would make room for me. I completely forgot about that statement but I had someone saying I had to make a decision. Burned....

I was 2 minutes away from Tyler Perry. When I say I that includes my Sugarbear. A letter to God had just opened up new doors ....

We made the wrong decision..... we should have stuck to our guns went for the stage. The door opened and we had the opportunity to change lives through the stage but instead we were tricked out of dreams and aspirations.. well one huge part of them because we are still writing our books...

BURNED

If we had a second chance we would choose what was and is best for us and not give validation to another man's beliefs for our lives...

Once he came through the door his aroma hit me and I knew it was a dream come true! It was so strange because I was the only one that could smell him...

It was reality TV on 100!

BURNED

MURDER GONE WAY TO SOON NOT AGAIN WHY GOD WHY? I CANT DO IT AGAIN NOT MY BABY HES JUST A BABY TAKE ME INSTEAD HE DIDN'T DESERVE TO GO LIKE THIS I NEED HELP GOD ON THE NEWS AGAIN JUST LEAVE ME ALONE HELPPPPPPPP

October 2015 complete devastation, my entire world was shattered, my heart ripped apart shattered in a million parts across the world.. My baby boy was meet by a hit and run driver!

BURNED

Not only did he hit him but looked in his rear view mirror and watched as other cars drove over his broken body. He took away a major part of my life, heart, breath, soul, love, joy, peace, smile, spirit... my baby...

BURNED

The killer laughed in my face again... I refuse to loose anyone else to the killer...

He was a great human being with flaws just like everyone else but I didn't care about them. What I cared about was his smile, the way he made me laugh when I was going through and didn't know where to turn on life's highway.. he provided a sense of security and unconscious unconditional love for everyone. But of course he was a part of me. He used what I gave him and he completely gave it back to me.

BURNED

By the time I got to him he had already taken flight..

HE WAS FREE NOW….. no more hurt pain, asthmatic, disappointments, bills, breathing treatments….

BURNED

I keep asking why didn't someone pray for him and with him it might have given me time to see him with breath in his body. I finally realized I would have made a mess of the master plan.

Listen the lady that held him as he took his last breath did the write thing, she prayed the prayer of salvation with him and let him know that I loved him. He repented and gave his last breath. My solider! My hero! My heart! Pain free....

The whole time Sugarbear never left my side, he stuck to me like glue to ensure that I would not give up, in or out. He even did the eulogy, my uncle was supposed to come but at the last minute he said he couldn't get here. Burned again...

As I looked around I was surrounded with his dads entire family, I didn't have one person from my family in the building.

I had four people that I considered my family in the middle of the of the storm. My two sisters from world of faith, Von and Bobbie, and my new found family that took care of myself and Pastor Tony and the children. Prophetess Hightower and Prophetess Shaunte.

My beautiful Jamaican sister Debbie brought me and Dante's favorite meal curry chicken and white rice, Hightower brought oven baked spaghetti, salad, with drinks and more, we had food for days already but listen These two sisters can throw down in the kitchen.

Now every event we had Pastor Tony, myself and Hightower would prepare the food.. our children also participated in everything we did.... they were the praise team, dance Ministry, ushers, pastor assistants and event staff.....

BURNED

Every child that lived in the house at that time gave me strength and love without equivocations. I always had someone by my side night and day. They made sure that I ate and took my meds because I lost myself when Dante left.

I mean I had talked to him not even a week before he went home. He told me that he loved me and I told him you know I love you and I could hear him smile. He wanted me to tell everyone he loved them and I started telling everyone he loved them. And few days later I get the dreaded call... I couldn't hear see or fathom what was going on....

Omg... I just... I am completely grateful for the opportunity that God gave me with Dante... for those that didn't know Dante was spoiled rotten... every time he asked me to go somewhere I would take him, if wanted money or Van's he knew exactly what to say to get what he wanted. He was very respectful and his smile said it all... now don't get me wrong he skipped school and did silly teenager stuff but that doesn't make him no worse than anyone else.

Dante knew how to make me smile and everyone else that he was around. He loved his new family, he gained when me and Sugarbear got together, he thought he was the younger children father lol. When they did wrong he would have a stern conversation with them, he took them and brought them candy and junk food when I'd say no junk food. Eventually someone spilled the beans...

I was so nervous but extremely excited when me and Sugarbear, and Tony Jr. Took him to get his license. Sugarbear was teaching everyone in the house to drive but Dante got his license first then Tony jr.

Now these two were in charge when Sugarbear and I were gone...they ran a tight ship.... it's so much I can say but I'll move on....

BURNED

So long for now, I'll see you on the other side my son!

THANK YOU FOR ALL MY FLOWERS AND CANDY AND HUGS, LOVING ME, BEING THEIR FOR ME IN GOOD AND BAD TIMES...

BURNED

Listen when you have gone through desert storm you learn how to function different. You don't have time to fight, fuss, or fall into arguments. You learn how to remain calm in the middle of every battle you face and not show your behind. Your walk is different so is your language. You know longer need to plant bitter seeds.

For those that have been and are still living in a bad relationship you have to determine what you really want from the other person and they have to do the same.

You both have to be on one accord and do whatever is best for you. Listen you can't let what people say dictate your life. Only you and God knows truly know's what is best for you.

You have to seek God in all that you do. Sometimes the outside world wants to be completely miserable just like them. I say you don't. You have a choice, raise your voice and be heard.

You certainly don't have go through 20 years of hurt or humiliation or being treated like an endangered species. You have the right to live a life full of joy, peace and happiness full of love!

My story doesn't end here, my life is just beginning...I overcame sexual abuse as a child. As a semi adult I overcame domestic violence, depression, oppression, suicidal thoughts, self inflicted pain, and addiction to foolishness!

It took awhile but I did it. I had the amazing support of my new husband and counseling.

BURNED

By the way counseling outside of ministry, church can be very effective along with prayer and fasting. It's up to you to decide what is best for you. You should never allow anyone to dictate what is best for you. Only God knows what is best for you, and if you seek him he will tell you what is best for you.

As an adult I have become a better person who's no longer bitter about the things life has brought me. I'm no longer ashamed of my past and where I came from to get where I am now. Now a few years back I can admit to the fact that murder was on my mind hate was in my heart along with so much bitterness. I couldn't shake the dust off my body nor numb the pain it was just undeniably hard... the sleepless nights the bucket of running water from my eyes... the steaming hot showers that I somehow thought would wash the filth that was inflicted upon me and even the self inflicted pain.

I had no choice but to seek counseling because it was so heavy and it got to the point where nothing else was helping me. I mean I was on the verge of a very serious meltdown. I was about to end it all. My mind body and soul were tired and confused... I mean praying didn't help, being in church every time the doors were open, listening to gospel music all the time, being in the prayer line didn't bring me relief... I was screaming to the top of my lungs and not one sound was coming out. I mean I never asked for this life it was give to me. I didn't understand my navigation system until the second phase of life. Now that I'm older and wiser I'm greater because I know how to function differently. I'm extremely thankful for counseling because I'm in a better head space..

I'm extremely grateful for my blended family and how each one push me beyond myself.

I definitely love all 11 of my blessings called children even though they all at some point get on my nerves.

BURNED

I just want them to do something so amazing. I want them to step outside of themselves and see what I see.

Potential, they all have it and sometimes I feel like fear is holding them in bondage. They can go so much further if they would just listen to the voice of wisdom and knowledge and stop acting like they know everything.... I have no shame cause I know some of y'all feel the same way....

In fact some of you need to hear from wisdom and knowledge.... we all do at times.

Just in case you didn't know, me and my Sugarbear are rock solid. As long as we stay in our word, we pray and fast together, we study together we gonna be together until death do us part. At any rate whom God joins together no man can separate!

I made the decision to tell my story to be a blessing to someone else who dealt with and may be dealing with the same type of issues I faced in the past so they can make a clear decision about their own future.

This was book was written SIMPLY to assist in my healing process. Remember never judge a book by its cover because it will definitely have you in the dark looking for the light switch.

I believe that I became a better version of myself, I learned to love and love back without any equivocations.! I'm a better listener and I no longer sit at the judgment table. I give the world around me the opportunity to look beyond my fault and love me for me. I truly appreciate my family and those in my extremely small circle.

I even enjoy my freedom from religion, other peoples concept of me and what they feel like I should be doing and not doing. I have truly learned to love me just the way I am flaws and all.

When God opens up the door for your walk through it and own it. Stand tall and don't deny your blessings.... you deserve the absolute best no matter what your circumstances are.

BURNED

Just a reminder, along the way you may encounter potential counterfeits but if you hold fast to the word your true mate will come when you least expect it, it may be a week from now or two years from now, or it could possibly someone right underneath the tears you have cried and not payed attention to that's watching and waiting for the stage doors to open and make an entrance. Listen dreams do come true. You just make sure that your focused on your destiny and not desire. Your desires will come.....

Now everyone doesn't heal the same way, I submit to you that we all have a healing process and this is my process. Listen never judge someone's process because you could be dealing with the same warden or worse. I know people that have died at the hands of their oppressors and I don't want that to be your final chapter, I want you to come out of the fiery furnace like pure gold untouched with no smoke residue. You are stronger than you feel and think!

I pray for your divine healing and that you would take control of your life. I pray that you trust God so much nothing else matters. Whatever your situation know that if I came out Alcatraz you can do the same, your not facing life in prison nor are you facing death row. God has given you a way to escape!

No matter what seat your in or how far you are away from your destiny know that you are a champion and no weapons formed against you shall prosper!

A few key things for you to remember is to never talk about your personal business to anyone unless you really can trust the person your confiding in. Just keep the nosey folks outside trying to peek inside your window. Not everyone is for you! Amen!

BURNED

Thanks

I want to take the time out to say a special thank you to my husband and my best friend for all the encouragement and support he gave me as I put pen to paper.

I thank you for standing with me during the sleepless nights, the nightmares, the frustration, countless hours of counseling and praying me thru... even when I wanted to throw in the towel and say forget it...

You know when you're going in the jungle you have to a strong sidekick and a warrior with you. Well my warrior had the full armor of God on and would not back down for nothing. He held on to my secrets just like they belonged to him and for that I'm extremely grateful.

He pushed and pulled me through the most difficult and frustrating times of my life as he held me tighter than a hogtied pig on a farm. He spoke so eloquently into my spirit with power and authority. He covered my nakedness and blocked me from myself. He continues to hold me accountable for my actions and responsibilities, I haven't heard not one judgmental statement nor one accusation.

I am fortunate and forever grateful for the opportunity to be connected with greatness and equality!

I love you my Sweet Sugarbear!

NOW CAN I HAVE SOME ICE CREAM?

BURNED

BURNED

Now for my new and old readers, I want to thank you for taking the time out to join me as I traveled up and down life's highway.

Many of you are unsure of what you want and what you're looking for from life and have veered off into uncharted territory. I want you to realize your not alone and you have to reflect, and redirect your thoughts and get back in the game of life with a new found focus, learn to love yourself, let go and let God love you, and then you can begin the healing process.

So many people judge us just from the title around our necks and completely forget about all the colors on our sleeves. Please don't be tangled up in the web of deceit. and become hypocritical when you haven't submerged yourself in the waters on these pages...

I love you all so much and thanks for traveling with me as we begin to open up and start the healing process.

BURNED

THANK YOU JESUS!!!!!!

THANK YOU FATHER GOD FOR MY LIFE HEALTH AND STRENGTH! THANK YOU FOR THE JOY OF MY SALVATION. THANK YOU FOR BEING MY LIGHT IN THE DARKNESS, THANK YOU FOR MEETING MY EVERY NEED AND REMOVING MY FEARS AND DOUBT. FATHER YOU HAVE BEEN SO KIND TO ME. YOU KEPT ME FROM DEATH AND OTHER TRIALS. YOU HAVE SHOWED ME GRACE AND MERCY EVEN WHEN I WASN'T BEHAVING YOU GAVE ME CHANCE AFTER CHANCE.. I'M JUST SO THANKFUL FOR ALL YOU HAVE DONE FOR ME IN SEASON AND OUT OF SEASON IF I WANTED IT OR NOT. I THANK YOUR FOR ALL THE TEACHERS IN MY LIFE GOOD AND BAD!
OH MY GOD IF I HAD TEN THOUSAND TOUNGS I COULDN'T THANK YOU ENOUGH!

I GIVE YOU ALL THE GLORY AND HONOR THAT'S DUE UNTO YOU NOW AND FOREVER MORE!

BURNED

BURNED

A special thanks to Bishop Anthony and Charlene Hatcher for being wonderful leaders and teacher of the Gospel of Jesus Christ for you have been great examples. Thank you for taking the time to nurture my gifts and push me into my destiny. Thank you for believing in me and being my support system!

BURNED

BURNED

Last but certainly not least I say thank you Dr. Pamela Robinson for rocking with me through the second part of my journey. You have been a true inspiration and influence in my life. You are a true representative of a woman of distinction, grace, love, integrity, wisdom and strength! Your love and blessings me the world to me and Tony.... you took us in when we were thrown to the wolves and stood in the gap as a real mother. You washed our faces, clothed us and feed us, you nursed us back to life and health. You spoke into our hearts and let us knew that we belonged and we had so much work to do and encouraged us to take charge of our lives and to keep moving forward no matter the looks on the faces in front of us looked like. I can speak for myself and Tony.... we are eternally grateful and blessed to have you in our lives.

BURNED

BURNED

BURNED

www.ingramcontent.com/pod-product-compliance
Ingram Content Group UK Ltd.
Pitfield, Milton Keynes, MK11 3LW, UK
UKHW051207260726
13967UKWH00011B/3152